You
Know
You're

50

When...

RICHARD SMITH
Illustrated by Debra Solomon

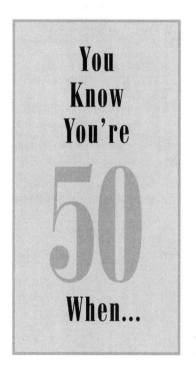

You
Know
You're
50
When...

Special Large Print Edition

BROADWAY BOOKS • NEW YORK

Library of Congress Cataloging-in-Publication Data
Smith, Richard, 1942 April 23–
    You know you're 50 when . . . / Richard Smith ; illustrated by Debra Solomon.
  —Special lg. print ed., 1st ed.
    p.   cm.
  ISBN 0-7679-0210-6
  1. Middle age—Humor. I. Title.
[PN6231.M47S6   1998]
818'.5402—dc21   97-47071
                                          CIP

Designed by Pei Koay

  01 02 20 19 18 17 16 15

You Know You're 50 When . . .

* *

"You're only as old as he feels."
—51-year-old divorcée discussing her new personal trainer

How do you know when you're approaching 50? For most of us, it's simple, like consulting a birth certificate or realizing that, lately, it's taking a bit longer to touch up those roots. For others, it's more subtle—like growing misty-eyed upon hearing the Beatles sing "Yesterday" or trying to recall where your gum line was the day Nixon resigned. Happily, however, reaching 50 is not so bad. Not only does it mean you survived your forties, but it confers certain privileges. You get to do really cool things, like join the AARP, drape a natty afghan over your shoulders when you feel a chill, and spend your kids' inheritance on cruises, trips to Paris, and liposuction. Wrinkles now become "laugh lines," and, best of all, tactful friends start putting only one candle on your birthday cakes, thus sparing you the effort of blowing out fifty at once.

Actually, deciding whether you're 50 is easy. Determining which type of 50 you are—Typical (the blood rushes to your head when you try to open a stuck window) or Youthful (you still watch MTV, but in wingtips)—may be a problem. We hope these pages will help.

You Know You're 50 When . . .

- The first man you slept with is now collecting social security.

- Unless you've been knighted, you want to smack people who call you "sir."*

- You're shocked to discover that "Chemical Peel" isn't the name of a stripper.

*Exceptions:
  - The doorman
  - Your daughter's date for the junior prom.

• On your second honeymoon you tip the bellhop extra to carry her over the threshold.

You Know You're 50 Pop Quiz #1

1. You gloated over how old Arnold Schwarzenegger looked in his last movie:

    Yes_____ No_____

2. You rejoiced over how young Sean Connery looked in his last movie:

    Yes_____ No_____

- Your therapist starts calling you for advice.

- You finally get your own apartment.

- The "good" side of the bed is the side closest to:
  - The bathroom
  - the humidifier.

- "Hip huggers" refer to cellulite.

- You're on your fourth dog.

• You ask for your will and an eraser when your daughter gives you a "Dancin' Grampies" exercise tape for Christmas.

• You're considering a move to a gated community (and buying a Ford Crown Victoria).

• Digesting Hungarian goulash without incident makes you believe there might be a Higher Power.

• You wonder how Mick Jagger stays so thin.

• You wish *Modern Maturity* instead of *Penthouse* arrived in a plain, brown wrapper.

Symptoms and Signs

Q. How do I tell if I'm undergoing a midlife crisis?

A. Check your garage:

Yes if it now contains   **No if it still contains**

A new Porsche 911*   Your trusty Buick LeSabre

*And the au pair.

- You drop off your dry cleaning at the post office.

- You forget your mantra.*

- At noon you begin planning your wardrobe for the "Early Bird Special."†

- A sign proclaiming "No Services Along This Route" makes your bladder panic.

*Not a problem if your Yoga teacher has a pager.
†Applies only to those who've taken early retirement.

• A mug that says "To the Best Grandpa in the World" induces a 4-day depression.

- You remember when people still snickered at the concept of bottled water.

- You actually start to obey the "Don't Walk" signal.

- "Performance anxiety" refers to golf.

- Your wife offers to help you change a flat.

Putting Your Age on Hold

If you have good genes and exercise regularly, you can remain 50 years of age for many, many years. Why say you're 57, for instance, if you appear to be a radiant 49? Determine how old you look versus how old you actually are with the following scientific formula (the same used by top Hollywood agents for their star clients):

$$\frac{NOH}{AOS} + JSF \times HOC = APF$$

*In which NOH (Number of hairs on head) divided by AOS (area, in inches, of your scalp) plus JSF (Jaw-Sag Factor) multiplied by HOC (height of cheekbones) equals APF (age you can pass for). Additional examples:

Real Age	How Old You Can Pass For If You
48	Are at your perfect weight, have 87% of your hair and perfect teeth: 40 to 45
51	Tan without burning: 41 to 45

Real Age	**How Old You Can Pass For If You**
50	Regularly eat a nourishing breakfast: • Bran with skim milk: 44 • Grapefruit, cornflakes and Ovaltine: 43 • Herbal tea with baby back ribs: 70
54	Work out regularly: • Jog: 45 to 49 • Power walk: 43 to 47 • Commute: 58 to 61
52	Have a family history of: • Warm, loving closeness: 41 to 44 • Not speaking to each other: 57 to 66
53	Possess great genes: • Father alive, over 85: 44 to 47 • But doesn't recognize you: 53
54	Have easily survived any of the following life crises: • End of a relationship: 47 to 49 • Cat pees on new Aubusson: 50 to 53 • ¼ share in a summer house: 48

• You try to outdo your friends' backache stories.

- It can take up to 15 minutes to climb out of a hammock.

- You call 911 to get you out of the Lotus position.

- You change a fuse, you feel it the next day.

- The two excuses most often used for not having sex:
  1. "We're saving ourselves for our second honeymoon."
  2. "We'll wake each other."

• That 7-year itch turns out to be eczema.

"The trouble with boy toys is that they always want you to put them through law school."

—Woman of a certain age

- If they ask, you tell your kids you never:
  - Inhaled
  - Could afford it
  - Could roll one properly.

• You and your partner resolve the "empty nest" syndrome by becoming lovebirds.*

• Your wife feels something go bump in the night; it isn't, alas, you.

• You put on reading glasses to listen to books on tape.

*Recurring sexual fantasy among happily married couples over 50: Is our money working hard enough for us?

• When reading the obituaries you don't care who died, it's how long they lived.

• Before getting together you no longer ask blind dates to fax you a financial statement.

• You hope eating less red meat will cut down on liver spots.

• You start calling your middle son by your youngest son's name.

- Your favorite sex position is both on the bottom.

• You buy an Airstream.

• After a go-to-hell Sunday brunch of eggs, toast (with 2 pats of butter), home fries, corned beef hash, and two orange blossoms, you finally make contact with your inner self (false alarm—they were gas pains).

• "Incontinent" no longer refers only to a major land mass.

• Your sexual fantasies include a Domino's pizza with everything on it. (Note: 17% of people over 50 report having a near-death experience after eating an anchovy pizza.)

- You blank when you try to recall:
  - Your social security number
  - Why you're standing in front of an open refrigerator.

- You swear you'll never own:
  - A pill counter
  - Support socks.

- You start believing that laugh lines are distinguished.

- "Al dente" refers to Tums.

- That invitation to join AARP makes your heart sink (how'd they know?).

• You start jogging with ID.

• You're shocked to suddenly realize that "Masters" applies to you!

• Your children now earn salaries, not an allowance.

• At your high school reunion you carefully clock your classmates for signs of aging.*

• Lately you've been wondering how you'd look driving a Winnebago.†

*And note with satisfaction that the high school sweetheart who broke your heart is 40 pounds overweight and missing several important teeth.
†With a bumper sticker stating, "We're spending our kids' inheritance."

• You now select hats for their SPF factor (the more silly-looking, the better.)*

*Fashion tip: diameter of the brim should not exceed 4 feet.

• You associate kidney-shaped pools with passing a stone.

• "Twice a night" now refers to bathroom visits.

• After six months of dating, your new girlfriend looks deep into your eyes and says, "I want you to be the grandfather of my grandchildren."

• You're up to 2.75 on your reading glasses. (But at restaurants vanity prevents you from using them to study the menu and you end up ordering baked lox au gratin.)

• You vow never to be caught playing shuffleboard.

• Without asking, the flight attendant hands you a blanket when you board the aircraft (extra-insulting if the plane is Bahamas-bound).

• You're still able to recall where you left your keys but not what they unlock.

• Not only do you know who Perry Como is, you also know which song made Johnny Ray famous.

("The Little White Cloud That Cried.")

• You now read *Playboy* for the fashion tips.

• A bad hair day pertains to those growing out of your nose.

- Women under 30 consider you:
  - Cute
  - Nonthreatening.

- Your wife sees no difference when you suck in.

- You fondly recall when "a dollar's worth" got you three gallons of Hi-Test.

- You remember when Exxon was Esso.

• Spending your mornings combing a beach with a metal detector doesn't sound too bad.

At-a-Glance Longevity Guide–Part I

Stressful events that could affect how long you live.

Discovering first	From your life subtract
Wrinkle	3 hours
Crow's foot	5 hours
Gray hair	4 hours
Bit of unwanted flesh*	1 day
Cellulite	8 hours
Age spot	2 days
Droop	6 hours
Sag	7 hours
Nagging backache	1 day
Heartburn	2 hours
From Tex Mex	5 hours
From bad haircut	8 hours

*Like a colossal love handle.

- You blame impotence on barometric pressure.

- At last it's okay to sleep late, but you can't.

- You re-find religion, just in case.

- You again start having single friends to fix up.

- You can't recall lending them when your neighbor returns your:
  - Weed whacker
  - Wife.*

*Especially disturbing if you also can't recall what they're used for.

- You flirt with writing an autobiography.

- You panic and call the optometrist when your wife gets that gleam in her eye.

- It takes an extra two days to digest your beloved spouse's macaroni casserole.

- Your kids' trust fund is going for:
  - Pec implants
  - A tattoo.

• While visiting your aunt at the nursing home you're mistaken for one of the residents.*

*Applies only to those who smoke 4 or more packs a day.

- "Substance abuse" means sweet and sour pork.

- You know who Carnac was.

- You realize that French cooking is overrated.

- You order "The Duke" porcelain sculpture of John Wayne from the Franklin Mint.

• "After dinner speech" refers to the noises emanating from your digestive system. (Decorum tip: Mute the sound by wearing a sweater.)

Official Turning-50 Signs of Mellowing

1. You accept that you'll be called for jury duty till you die.

2. Instead of an assault rifle, you now express "road rage" with a water pistol.

3. You stop resenting them and start to think of taxes as a cover charge for life.

4. You make a point of remembering to put the seat down so your beloved doesn't drown.

5. You allow your husband to hold the TV remote.*

*Except during *Oprah*.

• An obscene phone call makes your day.

• You spot money on the sidewalk but refuse to bend over for anything less than $1.00.

• For medicinal purposes you finally start drinking the red wines you've been hoarding.* Longevity tip: Cardiologists praise particularly the cholesterol-lowering benefits of:

- Petrus (1994)
- Clos de Vougeot (1993)
- Chateau Haut-Brion (1993)
- Grand Echezeaux (1988)

• A slightly diminished belief in your own immortality makes you realize that time is getting precious . . . so you take more naps.

---

*Although a white Burgundy, the '89 Chassagne-Montrachet, has been found to significantly reduce arterial plaque by the FDA.

• You wish you also had the courage to be a bald man with a ponytail.

• Butter becomes a dirtier word than S——.

• "Moderation" means fewer cigarettes and more cigars.

• You think that a "mosh pit" is something found at the center of an exotic tropical fruit.

• You need glasses to find your glasses (see page 82 for further explanation).

- Your beloved garlic finally turns on you.

You Know You're 50 Pop Quiz #2

When a friend you haven't seen in a long while says, "Gosh, you look terrific for your age," you assume he is:

1. About to borrow money
   Yes_____ No_____

2. Being totally sincere
   Yes_____* No_____

3. Seeking a summer job for his son
   Yes_____ No_____

4. Networking
   Yes_____ No_____

* A "yes" indicates a healthy self-image.

• You start using a tea cozy.

• In addition to a Primary Care Physician, you have your very own cardiologist (and shamelessly drop his name at cocktail parties if he's prominent).

• Instead of your beloved cat, your wallet now contains a photo of your angioplasty.

• Your calculator overheats while you're figuring out (for the third time this week) how much you'll have when you retire.

• You start obsessing over who'll die first: you or your money.

Great About-to-Turn-50 Moments in History

"The clerk still demands ID when I buy cooking sherry."

—Linda, age 49

"When we snuggle, my wife loves the hair that's starting to grow on my back—it keeps her extra warm."

—Sid, age 49¹/₄

"On our second honeymoon I looked at my husband and realized (sigh) that all the good ones really are married."

—Eileen, 48

"I was beginning to panic, then I realized those hot flashes were just my husband's Nikon. He was photographing me for the Mrs. America contest."

—Vickie, age 50

"Okay, so they can't carry a tune, but I still appreciate the wolf whistle when I pass a group of construction workers."

—Candy, woman of a certain age

"Cellulite? What's cellulite?"

—Donna, wouldn't give us her age

• As a gesture of solidarity, the hairline on your high school yearbook photo starts to recede.

• You have no guilt about appearing in pajamas and flicking the lights on and off when it's time for dinner guests to leave.

• You wish your son would at last run away from home (he didn't get the hint when you gave him luggage and a car for his 30th birthday).

• You head straight for the "Relaxed Fit" section when you buy Gap jeans.

- Your nails start growing faster (it's the vitamin E).

- Frequency rate refers to how often:
  - The kids call to borrow money.
  - Your wife asks you to fix the faucet.

- You wish "the ol' ticker" had a quartz movement.

- You treat yourself to a new set of golf clubs.

• During idle moments, you wistfully wonder if it's not too late to become a Texas Ranger.*

*Or, if you prefer a more fashionable uniform, a Canadian Mountie.

FDA-Approved Post-Fifty Marital Aids*

(Items that have been shown to promote bliss in couples afflicted by the "blahs.")

1. Multivitamins—to increase the shelf life of a low energy partner

2. A diamond tennis bracelet (she's earned it)

3. Crisp, new, designer sheets—fitted so they cling to the mattress during torrid moments

4. A second honeymoon (ocean view preferred)

5. A hot tub

6. A fireplace

*Over-Fifty Bedroom Wisdom: When it comes to romance, past performance is no guarantee of future results.

7. Anti-oxidant pills (to prevent partner from rusting during bouts of prolonged lovemaking)

8. Never uttering the words, "backache," "headache," or "raincheck"

9. Champagne

10. Bifocals (to facilitate location of erogenous zones)

11. Cuddling

12. A "Do not Disturb" sign on the door (for couples who are not yet "empty nesters").

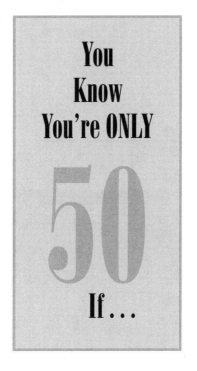

You
Know
You're ONLY

50

If . . .

- You still wear your decoder ring.

- You're not sure what you want to be when you grow up.

- You still use Clearasil.

- The prospect of a quiet evening at home drives you nuts.

- Your spouse still admires you for your body as well as your money.

- In the right light (either over candlelight, in an intimate French bistro, or the subway) you easily pass for 40.

- Quietly re-reading your husband's old love letters makes you blush.

- You'll still take a chance on a blind date.*

- Your parents want to know when you're going to give them grandchildren.

- You don't need to dim the lights when studying yourself in a full-length mirror.

- You still have some baby fat, even when you flex.

- You're not yet secure enough to ask directions when hopelessly lost.

*Unless it's a fix-up by your uncle in the carpet business.

- You still possess that sense of joyful, giddy spontaneity.*

- Quality time refers to "Happy Hour."

- You still resent your high school algebra teacher.

- You can do one-handed pushups without grunting (audibly).

- Your mistress still considers you a "boy toy."

- When taking public transportation, no one offers you a seat.

- You still do justice to bikini underwear.

*Your spouse doesn't need an appointment to have sex.

• You still get Valentine cards signed "Guess who?"

• Your "golden years" seem centuries away.

• You've yet to meet the food that doesn't agree with you.

• You're still on your first childhood.

• Unless it's at the Bali Club Med, the term "assisted living" makes you cringe.

• That immense, post-seafood gumbo burp doesn't shake any fillings loose.

Despite a friend's triple bypass you still partake of these 10 basic food groups:

1. Buttered corn muffins
2. Burritos
3. Spam
4. Egg rolls
5. Ice cream
6. Hash browns
7. Fried chicken
8. Prime ribs
9. Pecan pie
10. Cheesecake

• "Kicking up your heels" means lifting your feet so your wife can vacuum.

• You think the IRS should go easier on you.

• On your second honeymoon you bring an oxygen bottle.

• You've acquired the wisdom never to give your credit card number over the phone to a man selling:
  · Stucco siding
  · Time share condos on Okinawa
  · Juicers.

• You re-fall in love with your spouse.

You Know You're 50 Pop Quiz #3

1. You're considering having cosmetic surgery:
   Eyes done_____
   Neck tightened_____
   Complete face-lift_____
   Fuller, more generous lips_____
   Nose reconfigured_____
   Hair plugs_____
   New chin_____
   Bosom enhanced_____
   Stubborn love handles sucked_____
   Hip reduction_____
   Calf implants_____
   Legs waxed_____
   You-name-it_____

2. With money put aside to:
   a) Pay for your
      i) daughter's wedding Yes_____ No_____
      ii) son's bar mitzvah Yes_____ No_____
   b) redo the bathroom Yes_____ No_____

3. And you don't feel guilty
   Yes_____ * No_____

*Yes answer indicates a healthy sense of entitlement.

• You install grab bars in your bathroom.

- You need a larger safe-deposit box.

- You can recall when $1,000,000 was a lot of money.

- Instead of actually running the Boston Marathon . . . you figure what the heck . . . and take a cab.

- You carefully trim the fat from cookies.

Longevity Guide–Part II

Negative events that affect how long you'll live

Event	From your life subtract*
Smoking 1 pack a day	5–7 years
Bad news:	
In-laws coming to visit (with luggage)	4 days
Wrinkle cream fails	2 weeks
Paper cut	1 day
Attempting to make a connecting flight at O'Hare	16 days
A diet high in fat	5 years
Waiting for the next customer service rep	2 months
While listening to the Bee Gees	6 months
Favorite restaurant discovered by barbarians	10 weeks

*Figures are approximate.

Event	From your life subtract*
Parking attendant dings new BMW	19 days
Son needs another $22,000 for graduate school	1 year
Sticker shock	1 week
Remodeling your kitchen (unlicensed contractor)	4 years
Moving to a new home	2 months
Surprise visit by perky Welcome Wagon rep	5 months
Daughter's new fiance a rock drummer	47 weeks
Brother-in-law asks to borrow money for a waterbed franchise	9 months
More than 25 pounds overweight	2 years
Missing a hole-in-one by 3 inches	2 weeks
Drinking the white wine served at gallery openings	1 month
Maid quits without warning	6 weeks
Hemorrhoidal flareup	1 day
While changing a flat	1 week

• Blowing up balloons gets you winded.

• You vow to do something about your blood pressure (as your hand creeps into a second bag of "lightly salted" potato chips).

• You're starting to hoard (and neatly fold) shopping bags.

• Cops start letting you off with just a warning.

• Your allergies disappear.

- Taffy becomes an unreliable pleasure.

• A chewy bagel cracks a molar.

• Your wife catches you reading a "Hair Club for Men" brochure under the covers with a flashlight.

• You rediscover the joys of a perfect:
  • Summer day
  • Martini

• Those mysterious "UFOs" turn out to be spots before your eyes.*

*Or skydivers.

• When you stretch, you remain frozen in that position for 3 days.

- Minor loss of flexibility prevents you from:
  - Touching your toes
  - Reaching for the dinner check.

- "Smoking in bed" no longer refers (sob) to sex.

- "Alternative medicine" means Maalox.

- Instead of growing enraged, you relax and grab a nap when stuck in rush hour traffic.

• You sneak up to the attic to try on your old army uniform. (And get a hernia trying to close the jacket.)

- Friends no longer ask you to help them move.

- Standing up too quickly causes blackouts.

- Suddenly, *you're* the back seat driver.

- You'll risk sex in a hot tub only if there's a lifeguard present.

Symptoms and Signs

Q. Since turning 50, I occasionally have difficulty locating my reading glasses. Is my memory going?

A. Not to panic. Be reassured by the following chart.

If, when you finally find your glasses, they were	Indicates
In your pocket	You were preoccupied with more important matters, like the origin of the universe and whether to prune the ivy

If, when you finally find your glasses, they were	Indicates
Perched atop your head	A minor memory lapse, nothing to be concerned about unless you also can't recall what you were going to read
Suspended from a chain around your neck	A tad more than minor, but easily rectified by a diet high in fish
In your hand	Memory loss, merely a charming absent-mindedness, certain to endear you to a loving spouse
On your face	Lenses too clean

• At dangerous intersections, kindly strangers offer to help you cross the street. (Reward their impertinence by bopping them on the head with your cane.)

- Your children give *you* the curfew.

- You start using the pliers on your Swiss Army knife.*

- Staying power refers to remaining awake through *Cats*.

- You wish the school bus still brought you someone in desperate need of milk and cookies.

*To open those cursed bottles with a childproof cap.

Your main forms of aerobic exercise are:

Normal 50	Youthful 50	Elderly 50*
Tennis	Windsurfing	Checking your messages
Bowling	Sit-ups	Bingo
Fishing	Cycling	Checkers
Power walking	Cross-country skiing	Flossing
Gardening	Lifting weights	After-dinner naps
Deer hunting	Sky diving	**Feeding pigeons**
Squinting during cybersex	Jogging	Getting up to change the channel

*A condition easily reversed by running off with your secretary.

• At dinner parties, you fall asleep in your chair at 8 PM.*

*Not considered rude if:
  · No one notices
  · You cover your mouth when you yawn
  · You wear a sleeping mask.

• You begin to cherish those public displays of affection.*

• You start waving to strangers from your porch. (And get hostile if they don't wave back.)

• You cope with spring fever by planting marigolds.

• You think menopause entitles you to park in a handicap zone.

*Like a kindly stranger offering to press your floor on a dimly lit elevator.

You Know You're 50 Pop Quiz #4

1. Your ties are back in style.
   Yes____ No____

2. You've written to the Social Security Administration to request an estimated benefits statement.
   Yes____ No____

3. You know the difference between HDL and LDL.
   Yes____ No____

4. You've spent $3.95 on a "Wishin' I was Fishin' " bumper sticker.
   Yes____ No____

• After years of good living, your tailor diplomatically suggests it's time to let out your barbecue apron.

- You watch *Baywatch* for the plot line.

- Your son takes *you* fishing.

- Your mortgage payments are finally paying down the principal.

- You at last have the courage to ask your waiter to repeat the specials of the day . . . slowly and distinctly.

Longevity Guide-Part III

Positive events that can prolong your life.

Each Time You   To Your Life Add*

Buckle up for safety .... 3 hours

Substitute leafy greens for fried
catfish .... 1 week

Stimulate your intellect by
playing:
    Scrabble .... 5 hours
    Office politics .... 5 days

Achieve your target heart rate:
    On a treadmill .... 3 hours
    By dodging traffic .... 5 hours

Are recognized by an important
maitre d' .... 1 month

Get it wholesale .... 1 day
    From a designer show room ... 4 days

*Figures are precise.

Each Time You	To Your Life Add*
Discover the IRS owes you money	2 weeks
Stand up to your boss	2 days
Stand up to his secretary	1 week
Hug your teddy bear	5 hours
Leave work early to play golf	8 hours
Without getting caught	2 weeks
Think positive thoughts:	
The neighbor's dog will spare my geraniums	3 hours
This time they won't lose my luggage	5 hours
The plumber will say, "My treat."	1 day
They'll downsize someone else	2 days

• At the mall, you visit the information booth to find out where you parked your car.

- You still own a mechanical device that plays 45 rpms.

- You wish they made a low-fat, single-malt Scotch.

- You shop for an HMO that will cheerfully pay for a firmer jawline.

- You don't think it's funny when your wife plays "He loves me, he loves me not" with the remaining hairs on top of your head.

- You conserve energy by
  - Letting your husband mix the salad
  - Using an elevator to go up two floors
  - Pacing yourself when you shave
  - Buying a car with cruise control
  - Asking your wife to cut your meat
  - Walking around anthills.

Your Medicine Cabinet Contains . . .*

Pre-50

Toothpaste
Tylenol
Q-Tips
Mouthwash
Coppertone
Birth control pills
Midol
AA batteries (Walkman)

Thermometer
Handi-Wipes
Diaphragm (birth control)

Post-50

Polident
Doan's
Suppositories
Chicken soup
Grecian Formula
Tic Tacs
Prozac
Zinc batteries
(hearing aid)
Blood pressure kit
Depends
Diaphragm (memories)

*Skip this page if you're a youthful 50.

• You despair of ever learning a foreign language (like the metric system).

• On chilly nights, a nightcap is something you wear.

• You finally propose to your girlfriend of 21 years.

- You buy your first:
  - Hearing aid
  - Heating pad
  - Craftmatic Adjustable Bed.

• Your spouse installs a "choking victim" poster above the glass where you keep your dentures.

• Before catching himself, your dentist replies, "My daughter's Vassar tuition" when you ask how much work you need.

• You still can't forgive yourself for not buying Microsoft at 21.

• You have to aim extra carefully when dialing a touch-tone phone.

Turning-50 Magic Numbers

30: Number of seconds it takes to regain your composure the first time you're addressed as "madam."

17½: Number of heartbeats skipped when your daughter tells you that you're going to be a grandmother.

5: Number of days you walk on air when you try on last year's bathing suit and find it still fits.

4: Number of minutes you hunt for your car key before realizing it won't unlock the house.

28: Number of gray hairs you must discover before deciding it's time to see a colorist.

22: Number of times upper arms must jiggle* before tossing out your sleeveless dresses.

34,845,291: Number of women over 46 who don't mind being regarded as a sex object as long as it's by a) their husband or b) the pool boy.

*Condition reversible: achieve enviable upper arm definition by using husband as a free weight.

• The pin pricks in the lapel of your sport coat were made by a Jimmy Carter campaign button.

• Instead of compact disk, you now associate the letters "CD" with certificate of deposit.

• Anarchy means:
  · Buying a Harley T-shirt
  · Wearing it to Planet Hollywood.

- You hope it's your imagination when you notice:
  · An increase in shoe size
  · A decrease in height

Late Bloomer Alert

Is time getting shorter? Hardly. You have at least 35 more good years (45 years if you exercise regularly and avoid pork rinds). Consider a career change—to something more romantic and adventurous; a new profession that will bring out the maverick in you. Our career expert's suggestions:

▶

From (Current occupation)	To (Appropriate transition)
Butler	Body guard
Tailor	Surgeon
Truant officer	Bounty hunter
Toll collector	Repo man
Meter maid	Store detective
Banker	Black Jack dealer
Pearl diver	Navy Seal
Urologist	Gunsmith
Lawyer	CIA operative
Aerobics teacher	Bouncer
Politician	Maitre d'
Chemist	Bartender
Actor	Waiter
Psychiatrist	Psychic friend
Evangelist	Lounge singer
Computer programmer	Disk jockey
Prison guard	Innkeeper
Unemployed	Retired

- Your favorite sex toy is your memory.

- She asks if you were at the original Woodstock.

- You're relieved if she doesn't want sex on the first date.

• Instead of a long, leisurely weekend, the term "hanging out" refers to the object spilling over your belt (not to worry, it's merely your "inner child" trying to get out).

The 50-Year-Old Brain (partial contents)

Left Hemisphere

Taking pride in your accomplishments

Calculating how long until retirement

Fantasies about your masseur

Eating healthy

Undergoing corrective surgery to eliminate a double chin

Right Hemisphere

Wondering how face would look on a postage stamp

Wondering if you'll have enough money

Blushing

Cravings for Slim Jims

Dipping into the kid's college fund to pay for the new you

Left Hemisphere	Right Hemisphere
Starting your own business	Anxiety
Considering a new hairstyle	Possibly getting it spiked
Calling an old sweetheart	Collect
Realizing life's too short	To eat tofu burgers
Re-igniting love life	Coping with whisker burn
Vowing to improve golf swing	Hoping for a miracle
Planning a second honeymoon	Deciding whether to bring husband along

• Driving 16 miles to save 4¢ on a quart of milk makes your heart leap.

• Every chest twinge is, for sure, a heart attack.

• Your doctor is younger than you (and so is your therapist).

• You start to doublecheck supermarket receipts. (And lose a week's sleep if you think they overcharged you for the bananas.)

• Your carry-on luggage includes a defibrillator.

• You realize the next diaper you change may be your own.

• Florida starts looking good.

About the Author

Richard Smith plans to stay 50 for life.